What others are saying about *5 Life-Changing Prayer Principles*

Stu's heart for God and practical style make this book a great resource for all of us to go deeper in our prayer life with God. You'll find proven principles that will give you confidence to face your challenges and conquer your giants. Let Stu help you take your daily spiritual life to a new level in this fast-paced and Bible-based approach to effective prayer.

Garrett Booth, Lead Pastor,
Grace Church-Houston, Texas

Stu and I have been good friends for 50 years, and over the years I have often sought his counsel. It has always been wise and beneficial and most importantly, Godly. This book is a wonderful example of Stu's Spirit-led Godly counsel! Just this morning while walking our daughter's and son-in-law's dog, I used Stu's prayer model while seeking God's guidance on a major decision facing my wife and myself. How wonderful it is to experience more deeply God's purity, purpose, presence, power and protection!

Guy Gardner, Former Astronaut, Commander of the
USAF Test Pilot School, NASA Senior Executive,
and FAA Senior Official,
Locust Grove, Virginia

I had the privilege of endorsing Stu's book on leadership. In fact, I used this book in my School of Pastoral Nurture. His second book on 5 life-changing prayer principles is just as powerful as his first book. These 5 principles are based on over 40 years of prayer and listening to the Lord. Read and apply the principles, and your prayer life will be transformed!

Dr. Jack Hayford, Chancellor, The Kings University,
South Lake, Texas

Stu Johnson in his book 5 Life Changing Prayer Principles, sheds light on the most important event still to come in our future: The Second Coming of the Lord Jesus Christ. With those sober thoughts of being prepared, he challenges us to live a life of spiritual preparation, by connecting our devotional life to our prayer life. This book is a winner in helping you find practical ways to pray simple prayer principles that will change your life.

Mike Hooper, Senior Pastor of Church On The Lake in Livingston, Texas, & former Director of Prayer at KSBJ Radio and Prayer Pastor of Grace Community Church-Houston

Prayer is every believer's lifeline to God for intimacy with Him, for refueling our spirit, and for the provision that is needed to fulfill our mission. Stu Johnson doesn't give us a formula to follow but a foundation for the prayer life we need as we walk with God. I recommend this book to be included in the library of resources every believer keeps available for nurturing their spiritual life.

Tom Lane, Lead Executive Senior Pastor, Apostolic Ministry, Gateway Church, Southlake, Texas

I have served with Stu Johnson for more than five years as a fellow officer on The King's University board. He is a good friend and a seasoned leader with a huge heart for serving the kingdom of God. His new book, 5 Life-Changing Prayer Principles, is a must-read for both new and mature believers. This book can transform your prayer life!

Robert Morris, Founding Senior Pastor of Gateway Church & Bestselling Author Of *The Blessed Life, The God I Never Knew, and Frequency*, South Lake, Texas

Having known Stu as a ministry colleague for many years, also working alongside him in a leadership ministry assignment we both share, and having a deep friendship with strong accountability to each other, the principles he shares here come out of his experience in walking with God.   I know of no finer person you could learn these transforming truths about walking through the practice of prayer from, than Stu Johnson.

Dr. Steve Riggle, Founding Pastor, Grace Community Church-Houston & President of Grace International Churches and Ministries, Houston, Texas

5
Life-Changing Prayer Principles

5
Life-Changing Prayer Principles

Stu Johnson

with Bob Mimms

Optasia Books
PO Box 2011
Friendswood, Texas 77549

Copyright © Stu Johnson 2018

ISBN 978-194670821-2

Written in collaboration with Bob Mimms
and Karen Porter

Cover Art by © Pongsak Tawansaeng | Dreamstime.com

Cover Design by Maddie Scott

Optasia Books is an imprint of Bold Vision Books.
PO Box 2011, Friendswood, Texas 77549

Published in the United States of America.

Dedication

This book is dedicated to the countless people who have helped grow my prayer life. First, I want to thank Dave Malkin who prayed with me to receive the Baptism in the Holy Spirit and my prayer language. This prayer language has been incredibly helpful to my prayer life and growth. Second, I want to thank Pastor Don Van Hoozier. Pastor Don nurtured my wife and me in prayer for over 40 years, both in his presence and from a distance. He prayed for us countless times and modeled a strong prayer life. Third, I want to thank Pastor Paul Adams who did a series on the Lord's Prayer while we attended his church. The series was transformational for my prayer life. Next, I want to thank my wonderful wife, Debbe. She is my prayer partner and an incredible prayer warrior. Finally, I want to thank God for leading me and my wife to join or lead a number of home fellowship/prayer groups. These groups made corporate prayer much more comfortable and helped me to be more transparent in my sharing and prayers.

I cannot close this dedication without thanking the Holy Spirit who has been my ultimate prayer guide and teacher. All the principles in this book come from times of teaching or revelation from the Holy Spirit. In His love and goodness, I have experienced transformation in my prayer life. I thank you precious Holy Spirit.

Table of Contents

Introduction

"So stay awake, alert. You have no idea what
day your Master will show up"
(Matthew 24:42 The Message).

Staying alert on the road late at night after a long trip is difficult. Sometimes at the end of a long trip, I fight sleep and exhaustion. I've discovered some secrets to help me stay awake. I drink coffee. I turn the air conditioner to cold and the music to loud. I sing along with the radio and sometimes I stop the car at a rest stop so I can walk around for a while. All these methods wake up my senses and help me stay alert for anything on the road ahead.

Jesus told us to be alert and awake as we live on this earth, watching for His return and watching for opportunities to witness or to grow spiritually.

Not long ago, as a warm Texas-summer morning dawned, I began my daily Bible study on the topic of the day, the Second Coming of Christ—not prayer, but a topic that would lead to the crafting of this book.

An insight emerged from my study that was as profound as it was simple, a message that became urgent in my heart. *Time is thundering toward its prophesied end, but few see the lightning.* At a time when believers should be most aware, too many are spiritually asleep and numb to the growing storm.

Daily newscasts and headlines detail the pain and evil in modern life. Indeed, we are inundated by the heart-rending images and overwhelmed by the toll on life and spirit exacted by war, natural disasters, terrorism, blurred, if not shredded, morality, corruption in politics and business, mass shootings, disease, and starvation.

Have we become deaf to the drumbeat of history's final march? The signs are unrelenting and the indications are getting louder—as Christ and his apostles warned us it would. Still, too many of us seem too content to live in spiritual twilight, as if we are falling asleep at the wheel.

When Jesus spoke about his return, he said, "But concerning the day and hour no one knows, not even the angels of heaven, nor the Son, but the Father only…Therefore, stay awake, for you do not know on what day your Lord is coming. But know this, that if the master of the house had known in what part of the night the thief was coming, he would have stayed awake and would not have let his house be broken into. Therefore, you also must be ready, for the Son of Man is coming at an hour you do not expect" (Matthew 24:36, 42-44 ESV).

Some years later, the apostle Peter repeated the warning, underscoring the need for vigilance by the believer. "But the day of the Lord will come like a thief, and then the heavens will pass away with a roar, and the heavenly bodies will be burned up and dissolved, and the earth and the works that are done on it will be exposed" (2 Peter 3:10 ESV).

The Apostle Paul also used the Lord's nighttime intruder metaphor for watchful spiritual preparation: "Now concerning the times and the seasons, brothers, you have no need to have anything written to you. For you yourselves are fully aware that the day of the Lord will come like a thief in the night. While people are saying, 'There is peace and security,' then sudden destruction will come upon them as labor pains come upon a pregnant woman, and they will not escape. But you are not in darkness, brothers, for that day to surprise you like a thief. For you are all children of light, children of the day. We are not of the night or of the darkness. So then let us not sleep, as others do, but let us keep awake and be sober" (1 Thessalonians 5:1-6 ESV).

As I read these verses and contemplated the idea of being alert, some harsh realities smacked me between the eyes. First, most people—including many, perhaps most believers—will miss the signals of the most anticipated event of Christianity. Too many of us won't be ready.

Second, many of us have become focused almost entirely on living—not anticipating Jesus' return. Life has a way of consuming us, of sucking the energy out of us, if we let it.

Jesus warns, *Stay awake. Be prepared. I'm coming when you don't expect it.*

I was not looking for a new assignment or mission from the Lord. But I asked, "Lord, what can be done to help people get ready for your coming?"

I heard his answer in my mind, "The best way to be ready is to be devotionally connected to me. Teach them what I have taught you in your devotional life, particularly your prayer life."

I recalled some of the insights and practices the Lord has poured into my life concerning intentional, Bible-directed prayer. I had assumed everyone could and did practice these holy habits, but I realized most Christians have little or no prayer life.

That morning I began to put together this book as a tool and guide to help Christians enrich and empower their prayer lives.

It's been said that prayer changes things. The real truth is that prayer changes us. Prayer is for our good and prayer connects us with God. Rich, deep, meaningful prayer includes focusing on Him, listening to Him, praise, worship, thanksgiving, and agreeing with God not for what we want but for His will. According to John 9:3, the primary purpose of prayer is not to get what we want but instead "so that the works of God might be displayed...." God who is omnipresent—always present—hears us when we pray. God who is omniscient—all knowing—answers us when we pray. God who is omnipotent—all powerful—responds to our prayers.

As children of our heavenly Father, we do not make demands of God. Instead, we speak to Him in adoration, thanksgiving, and humility. Prayer can't be measured in a scientific way because sovereign God is in control, but believers don't approach prayer as if it is magic either. According to James 4:8, prayer helps us develop a deep relationship with God. "Draw near to God and He will draw near to you." God answers prayers. He intervenes. He rescues. He bestows blessings. He withholds. He gives.

> "Our prayers may be awkward. Our attempts
> may be feeble. But since the power of prayer is
> in the one who hears it and not in the one who
> says it, our prayers do make a difference."
> ~Max Lucado

In the following chapters, we will learn how to pray and become devotionally connected to the Lord. At the end, if you commit to embrace and practice these five principles, your life as a believer will be spiritually supercharged, blessed, and effective.

You will be *ready* for our Lord's return. Not surprised, not distracted or ashamed, but joyful with anticipation.

Together we will shine the spotlight on five principles of prayer: Purity, Purpose, Presence, Power, and Protection. These five words comprise the core of what I have practiced and pursued in my prayer life over the last 40 years. I use these five principles as the framework for my daily prayers. Every prayer seems to quickly fit under one of these words. In fact, this new framework seems to add new breath to my prayer life. As I've shared this new prayer-framework with small groups and congregations in the USA and overseas, the response has been incredibly encouraging as people put these prayer principles into practice.

I urge you to begin to use this framework in your prayer life, too.

1

Seeking His Purity

"God doesn't seek for golden vessels, and
does not ask for silver ones, but He
must have clean ones."
~ Dwight L. Moody

Long ago, the disciples asked Jesus to teach them how to pray. He answered with a template, which we call the Lord's Prayer (Matthew 6:9-13). You may have memorized this classic prayer in Sunday School and can still recite it, beginning with the words, *"Our Father, who art in heaven..."*

But chances are that we don't pray like Christ's model in word or tone. For most of us, if we are honest, our prayers are mostly about asking God for possessions that give us pleasure or comfort.

You know what I mean. *"God, help my family." "Oh Lord, I need a new job." "Help me deal with this." "God, please give me some money!"*

We're very good at prayers which ask for our desires, contentment, and happiness, but petition is not the main purpose of prayer. King David prayed, "Bend down, O Lord, and hear my prayer; answer me, for I need your help. Protect me, for I am devoted to you" (Psalm 86:1 NLT). David knew that his longings, aspirations, feelings, and motives didn't always meet the purity test so he asked God to help and to protect. When you read David's words in Psalm 51, it is clear that he craved purity that he couldn't accomplish on his own. "Wash me thoroughly from mine iniquity, and cleanse me from my sin" (Psalm 51:2 KJV). If a man who was described as a "man after God's own heart" needs to pray for purity, you and I should follow his example.

Purity is defined as clean, clear, virtuous, and honorable. Purity is not natural to humans. According to Romans 3:23, we have all sinned. Sin separates us from God, and we as humans are slaves to sin. The first prayer principle is to seek God's purity. The only way we will find purity is to pray like King David. Though he was King of Israel, David asked God to reveal the deepest parts of his heart, "Search me, God, and know my heart, test me and know my anxious thoughts" (Psalm 139:23 NIV).

I ask God to search my heart and reveal any sin.

On my "prayer walks" with my dog, I ask God to search my heart and reveal my sin. I'm on my fifth dog now. His name is Tucker, a St. Bernard-poodle mix. That's right, Tucker is a 60-pound St. Berdoodle—and he's heard this prayer so often that he could probably do it in dog language.

The first words out of my mouth as we begin our walk are, *"Lord, I ask you to search my heart. I give you permission to search my heart."* I don't dare pray anything else before I pray these words because the most important key to my relationship with God is that I open the doors to my heart to Him.

Is God going to discover anything in me that He already did not know? No—but He is going to show me what is in my heart. For many of us, blatant, flagrant sin isn't our biggest problem. Instead, we harbor feelings such as bitterness and unforgiveness in such deep places that we don't readily recognize their existence. Paul wrote about these deep-seated emotions in his letter to the Colossians. "But now you must also rid yourselves of all such things as these: anger, rage, malice, slander, and filthy language from your lips" (Colossians 3:8 NIV). Purity is found when God's light shines into the corners of our heart revealing every darkness that doesn't please God. King David added an additional phrase in the prayer, "Point out anything in me that offends You, and lead me along the path of everlasting life" (Psalm 139:23-24 NLT). When we pray for God to reveal all that is in our heart, He will show us the pure path to follow.

As I walk and pray, I lift a hand to the Lord. (I don't choke the dog; the leash is in the other hand. I don't worry about how it looks, either; people probably think I am exercising). My lifted hand represents my submission and my willingness to allow Him to shine His holy light on the shadowy parts of my heart. I pray, *Lord, search my heart. Look inside me for arrogance or defiance and for attitudes, opinions, and feelings that offend you. Highlight any stumbling block that will keep me from going through doors you open. Keep me from any action that will be a bad example to people. Bring sin to the surface; bring light on the darkness.* Since I have started praying this way, God has changed me, reminding me about attitudes that I need to correct and showing me sinful attitudes or actions. I marvel at the steps of repentance He has revealed.

I welcome His correction and instruction into my life.

When we pray for God to search our hearts, we are acknowledging God has the right to *spank* us. I know corporal is not a popular, politically correct concept, but God is not subject to the latest, self-obsessed behavioral indulgences of His creations. Out of His limitless love, He will *spank* us—to save us. But like a good Father, He will also instruct us.

There is a difference between instruction and correction, but the two concepts are related. In the Old Testament, the Hebrew word *musar* (רְסוּמ) is used 50 times, 30 times in the book of Proverbs alone. It was translated into English in the King James Version with various shades of meaning. In Proverbs 4:13 it is "instruction" to be taken in a firm grip, while Proverbs 3:11 refers to *musar* as "chastening" and "correction" not to be despised.

The concepts of *musar* extend to Christ. In Isaiah 53:5 (KJV), the prophet wrote that the Messiah would be *"wounded for our transgressions…bruised for our iniquities; the chastisement* (musar) *for our peace was upon Him, and by His stripes we are healed."*

God's instruction and correction as found in His Word means that as He educates and guides us, our responsibility is to read His Word, listen to His Holy Spirit, and seek to understand Him and follow Him. Praying for purity requires us to be teachable, coachable, and willing to hear Him and make the changes He expects.

Our prayer for purity must be, *Lord, I embrace instruction and correction, at any level You need to use. I welcome Your discipline, direction, as you train, coach, and transform me.*

I ask the Lord to grow me.

My prayer for purity continues, *Lord, change me and don't leave me as I am.* Asking God to *grow* us means we want Him to cultivate His nature in us, to strengthen His purity within us, and to transform us into the likeness of Christ. Asking for Christian growth is a conscious decision to live at the level of instruction where He speaks, and we obey.

Ask the Lord to develop godly character and spiritual fruitfulness. Galatians 5:22-23 (KJV) lists the "fruit of the Spirit" as *love, joy, peace, longsuffering, gentleness, goodness, faith, meekness* and *temperance.*

Memorize that list of the fruits of the Spirit, and begin now praying for these qualities by name. *Lord, grow me in love. Help me love the unlovable and those who have hurt me with words or actions. Fill me with joy no matter what my circumstances. Shower me with Your peace, especially when I'm stressed and overwhelmed. Give me patience with those who annoy me and with people who are slow to move or make decisions. Give me gentle words of kindness, and help me speak these words calmly and quietly. Pour Your goodness into me. Wrap me in the meekness of Jesus. Build my faith into a strong tower. Shape me into a person with self-control.* I have been praying for growth in this list of character qualities for more than 40 years. As I look back, I see tremendous growth and character transformation the Lord has produced through these prayers. For example, He has brought me to an incredible place of inner peace. For years, I wrestled with anxiety. Change threatened me. I think the core of the anxiety came from being raised in an alcoholic home. Yet God has transformed a life full of anxiety to a life blanketed in His peace.

The prayer for purity begins with asking God to examine my heart and continues when I listen to His instructions, heed His corrections, and allow the fruit of His Spirit to flourish and mature. Surrendering to His examination gives Him permission to expose sin, adjust attitudes, and then to teach, correct, rebuke and chastise us—whatever He needs to do for us to grow in godly character and service.

Not only do we need to remove what God reveals, we also need to add thoughts and attitudes that are pleasing to God. "Finally, brethren, whatsoever things are true, whatsoever things are honest, whatsoever things are just, whatsoever things are pure, whatsoever things are lovely, whatsoever things are of good report; if there be any virtue, and if there be any praise, think on these things" (Philippians 4:8 KJV). Pray that God will replace any evil thoughts, attitudes, views, opinions, and notions with purity. Pray that God will reveal truth and honesty to you in every situation. Pray for just, pure, lovely interactions in your life. Praise God. Consider virtuous ideals. Replacing impure with pure will radically change your life.

Don't be surprised when the changes God makes in you are like a total renovation you see on home makeover shows. He will take out all the parts of you that are undesirable. He may rewire you or make changes in the way you are framed. He will recondition, repair, restore, and even redecorate you. You will never be the same. It is transformation.

> "God is not the God of the tweak, He is the
> God of transformation."
> ~Garrett Booth

Reflections

Did this chapter challenge you to pray the prayer of purity?

What are your personal purity challenges?

Can you remember a time when you asked Him to reveal what area of your life needed His transformation? What happened when you prayed this prayer of purity?

How will you commit to asking God daily to search your heart and reveal areas that are offensive to Him or a stumbling block to you?

Read Hebrews 12:5-11. Name the benefits of God's discipline.

Have you asked God to grow you in character? What changes have you seen because of your prayers?

Have you every prayed for Godly character using the fruit of the Spirit? How has God changed your behaviors and attitudes because of the Holy Spirit's fruit?

2

Seeking His Purpose

"You were made by God and for God,
and until you understand that, life
will never make sense."
~Rick Warren

The number one question that believers wrestle with may be, "How do I know God's purpose and will for my life?" Young people want to know about their future. More mature believers want to follow God wholeheartedly. Yet the question is always there, "What is God's purpose for me?"

Seeing God's purpose is His intimate and personal call to each of us. He gives us the yearning to discover and pursue His unique vision for each of us. And when we uncover His dream for us, we can share, live, and grow in His love and truth through Christ.

Imagine when your time on earth ends and you stand before the Lord that you are shown a movie of your life. You want to see scenes where people were saved, blessed, healed, comforted, and encouraged through your obedience to God's purpose. You don't want to see all the missed opportunities. What we all long to hear are His words, "Well done, good and faithful servant; you were faithful over a few things, I will make you ruler over many things. Enter into the joy of your Lord" (Matthew 25:23 NJKV).

Dr. Charles Stanley said, "The Father's greatest desire is for you to have a relationship with Him through Jesus Christ.

Once you have received God's forgiveness, then you are ready to fulfill the rest of His plan for your life." The first question you must ask is whether you have a relationship with Jesus. Have you trusted Him as your Savior and Lord? Have you repented of your sin and turned your life over to Him? If so, you are ready to discover His purpose for you and follow His plan for your life.

In Jeremiah 29, the Lord speaks these words to us, "For I know the plans I have for you." So it is clear that God has a plan for each person. Then the Lord describes these plans, "They are plans for good and not for disaster, to give you a future and a hope" (Jeremiah 29:11 NLT). God has a good, hopeful, amazing, breathtaking plan for you and me.

How do we find that plan and purpose? Jeremiah continues, "In those days when you pray, I will listen. If you look for Me wholeheartedly, you will find Me. I will be found by you," says the Lord" (Jeremiah 29:12-14 NLT).

Jeremiah lays out the formula. It is **our** job to ask God to show us His purpose; it is **His** job to show it to us.

There are at least three steps that will help us ask God to show us His purpose.

Step 1: I present my body to Him each morning.

Pray this prayer, *"I belong to You. I am Yours. Lord, I want Your presence in my life. I present my body as a living sacrifice, holy and acceptable to God, which is my spiritual worship." (See Romans 12:1).*

In this prayer, we offer more than our "body," that creation of flesh, bone and blood that carries us—our spirit, our soul, our consciousness—around on this planet. Where would we be without that physical container, which Paul calls a "tent" in 2 Corinthians 5:1-4, to sustain and transport us?

When I pray this prayer, it means I am giving everything I am, physically and intellectually and spiritually, to God. My physical body: what I eat, what I see, where I go, how I exercise, how I rest. My mind: what I think, what I read and absorb, how I learn, how I believe. My spiritual self: who I trust, who I worship, how I connect with God. Am I willing to lay all of that down as a sacrifice to Him? My willingness to put every intricate part of me on His altar is my worship of Him.

The next verse in Romans explains how to offer the sacrifice. "Do not be conformed to this world, but be transformed by the renewal of your mind, that by testing you may discern what is the will of God, what is good and acceptable and perfect." (Romans 12:2 ESV)

The Message Bible paraphrases that passage in words Paul might use if he were preaching in today's vernacular.

"So here's what I want you to do, God helping you: Take your everyday, ordinary life—your sleeping, eating, going-to-work, and walking-around life—and place it before God as an offering. Embracing what God does for you is the best thing you can do for Him.

"Don't become so well-adjusted to your culture that you fit into it without even thinking. Instead, fix your attention on God. You'll be changed from the inside out. Readily recognize what He wants from you, and quickly respond to it. Unlike the culture around you, always dragging you down to its level of immaturity, God brings the best out of you, develops well-formed maturity in you" (Romans 12:1-2 The Message).

Presenting myself as a sacrifice to the Lord is a many-layered exercise and commitment...my body with all its requirements and needs, plus my mind with all its imaginations, and my spirit with its longings and cravings. My prayer continues, "Lord, I present You...me. I give You my body; I am acknowledging You own me. I am Your child; You are my Father. You are my King; I am Your servant."

This prayer begins our relational alignment, acknowledging that God is God, and we are not...seeking an intimate connection with our Father, and accepting His correction and cleansing as part of His indescribable, limitless, and all-encompassing love.

God can give us this kind of love because He is indescribable, limitless, and all-encompassing. *He is.* Moses asked what name he should call the Lord. God's response was,

"I Am" also translated as *"I Am that I Am,"* or *"I Am who I Am,"* or even *"I Am who I will be."* (See Exodus 3:14.)

God is everything you need at any moment. Like a blank check, signed and presented to you to fill in the amount. He is whatever you need whenever you need it. Let the awe of that promise permeate you. Have you ever gazed at a clear, star-filled night sky and been overwhelmed by the realization that each one of those lights is a sun, many bigger than and dwarfing our own? We see perhaps a few thousand stars with the naked eye, a tiny fraction of at least 100 *octillion* (that is a 1 with 29 zeros!) stars currently estimated by astronomers.

When I gaze at the stars, I am astonished because I am only one speck of dirt on a spinning pebble orbiting a 4.6 billion-year-old star. God made all the universe and more than we can comprehend. Yet, He sees us and loves each *one* of us, with a measure that is eternal—beyond even the ability of His universe to contain. *Infinite!*

Because of who He is and how much He loves me, I am compelled to lay my body, mind, and soul down on the altar as a living sacrifice to Him.

Step two, *I choose the fear of the Lord for my life.*

The Bible has dozens of references to the "fear of the Lord." Some passages show the positive side of the fear of the Lord and other passages reveal what happens when we don't fear the Lord. Proverbs declares that, "The fear of the Lord [is] the beginning of knowledge: [but] fools despise wisdom and instruction" (Proverbs 1:7 KJV). Later the wicked are described as those that "...hated knowledge, and did not choose the fear of the Lord" (Proverbs 1:29-30 KJV).

What the Bible calls the *fear of the Lord* is not a fear of panic or alarm but an awestruck fear of reverence and honor. The kind of respect and devotion brings you into the presence of the Lord.

Other verses promise blessing, protection, provision, healing, peace, and mercy for those who fear the Lord. The various Hebrew and Greek words translated as this *fear* convey attitudes ranging from deep respect to reverence and wonder.

I have personally witnessed this sort of *positive fear* at the death bed of a dear friend, when I was in my early twenties.

Ken was an older man with whom I had a father-son relationship. He developed a large aneurysm on his aorta artery, and I was visiting him in a Veterans Administration hospital. Near the end of the visit, Ken began to suffer pain in his chest. Doctors and nurses rushed in, and I held his hand as they tried to save him.

Within a few seconds, Ken sat up in his bed, reaching out toward something or someone I could not see. His face was filled with a mix of fear, awe, amazement and a great desire for what he reached toward. Ken's face captivated me.

I held his left hand, but suddenly Ken's outstretched right hand clasped, as if taking hold of another; then he fell backward onto his bed. As he collapsed, I heard a "pop" from his chest. Doctors later said that was the sound of his aorta bursting.

The Lord revealed to me that what I had seen on Ken's face was the *fear of the Lord*—no dread or terror at dying; only awe and wonder at seeing His Savior. Soon thereafter, my prayers started to include the declaration and plea to God: *"I choose to live my life in the fear of the Lord. Teach me about the fear of the Lord, and help me to think, speak, and live in the fear of the Lord."*

In addition to the lessons of Ken dying, the Lord later revealed to me in Proverbs 1:29 that one of the characteristics of the wicked is that they do not choose the fear of the Lord. I decided to choose the fear of the Lord as my life-compass every day in prayer. This choice is one of the foundation stones of my prayer life and means that I don't live in doubt or anxiety. Instead, I follow God who is able and willing to direct my path.

Over the years of studying and living this principle, I have become convinced the fear of the Lord is the critical underpinning of our Christian walk. In fact, on a prayer walk in 2004, the Lord asked me if I would like to see some of the blessings that came in my life because I had chosen this path.

As I reached the top of a hill, I opened myself to His offer. He showed me scene after scene from my life, blessings here, provision there, an open door to ministry, a relationship, one thing after another. After each scene, the Lord whispered, *"This happened because you chose the fear of the Lord...that happened because you chose the fear of the Lord."* The more He revealed, the more I felt in humble awe of His intervention in the details of my life.

If you want to find God's purpose and will for your life, tell Him how much you admire, respect, and esteem Him. Worship Him for the wonder of His love and mercy. Speak your amazement at how He cares for you. Pray in the fear of the Lord.

Step Three: I pray the prayer of Jabez, personally and for my family.

"And Jabez called on the God of Israel saying, 'Oh, that You would bless me indeed, and enlarge my territory, that Your hand would be with me, and that You would keep me from evil, that I may not cause pain!' So God granted him what he requested" (1 Chronicles 4:10 NKJV).

In praying for God's purpose, step three leads us into petitioning God for purpose that will make a difference in our world. Jabez asked boldly for God's blessings. He didn't mince words or try to polish up the rhetoric. Instead, he speaks straightforward, "Lord I want your blessings." Maybe your past or your shortcomings cause you to think that you don't deserve too much from God. But remember the words of Jeremiah 29:11 that promised good plans from God—plans to prosper and not to harm. It is time for you and I to pray for God to bring the blessings! *Lord we are ready and expecting Your best—because we know You only have the best awaiting us.*

Notice the next phrase of the prayer of Jabez. *Enlarge my territory.* In his book *The Prayer of Jabez*, Bruce Wilkerson explains that this part of Jabez's prayer is more than a wish for more real estate. In fact, it is a prayer for more opportunities and influence and the chance to make an impact on the Kingdom. As Wilkerson says, Jabez looked at his life and said, "Surely I was born for more than this." Let's consider how this part of Jabez's prayer works in our quest to find God's purpose for our life. We've learned in step one to lay all on the altar and in step two to live in awe of the one true God who performs miracles. Now God expects us to dream big, God-sized dreams. If our dreams are small, we don't need God. But big dreams need the intervention of the Creator of the universe, and when we trust Him enough for enlarged territory, He responds. "When you take little steps, you don't need God…but God always intervenes when you put His agenda before yours and go for it."

Ask God to enlarge your territory by giving you opportunities to witness, responsibility to care for someone, spaces to be kind, and occasions to show mercy.

The third part of Jabez's prayer is asking that God's hand would be with us. We want His guidance; we need His direction; we want to feel Him leading us into the paths that are planned for us. I love this part of Jabez's prayer and often envision His fingertips lightly touching my shoulders to direct my life.

The final part of Jabez's prayer is for the Lord to keep us from evil. I ask God to keep me from participating in evil or impacting others with any evil actions, words, or thoughts, thereby causing me or others pain.

"God's purpose is more important than our plans."
~ Myles Munroe

Reflections

What does "Lord" mean to you when you think about your relationship with Jesus Christ?

Does this word motivate or threaten you?

If you have never done so, are you willing to ask Jesus to sit on the "throne of your life right now"?

What thoughts or questions do you have about presenting your body to the Lord each day?

What do you think the benefits could be if you dedicated your body every day to the Lord, giving Him control of your life and purpose?

What are some of the purposes for your life that God has revealed to you?

Have you been living to fulfill those purposes?

In what areas do you want to see changes?

When you read about choosing the fear of the Lord, what were your thoughts?

How can you pray for this character quality in your life?

There are many promises that result from having the fear of the Lord in your life. What are some of them?

Read the "prayer of Jabez" again.

What are the four prayer requests that Jabez makes in this prayer?

Why could Jabez pray this bold prayer? Why can you also pray this bold prayer?

How does the phrase "enlarge my territory" affect your quest to find purpose?

Can you commit to praying this prayer every day?

3

Seeking His Presence

"I must first have the sense of God's
possession of me before I can have
the sense of His presence with me."
~Watchman Nee

The presence of God feels like a mystery. God is invisible and feels unknowable, but He is in Heaven watching over us, and He wants to converse with us. He is waiting, and prayer is the way He has chosen to communicate. Prayer is the key to His presence.

David understood the importance of God's presence especially because he yearned to be in the house of God. He said, "O Lord, I love the temple where you live, the place where your splendor is revealed" (Psalm 26:8). He longed for God's presence.

You may be a little confused when I use the term God's *presence* because we know the Lord is omnipresent—everywhere with no boundaries and with no limits in power or wisdom. Paul wrote that He is not far away, "so that they should seek the Lord, in the hope that they might grope for Him and find Him, though He is not far from each one of us; for in Him we live and move and have our being, as also some of your own poets have said, 'For we are also His offspring'" (Acts 17:27-28 NKJV).

As a believer and Christ follower, I want His presence more than anything else in my life. I ask for His presence to encompass me and envelop me; I want to live in His manifest presence.

I pray, *Lord, I want people to look at me and see You, to notice something different. Bathe me in Your name; write it on my mind and my heart.*

God has revealed His presence in many ways throughout humankind's sin-stained sojourn on a fallen Earth.

In Genesis, before Adam and Eve sinned, God *walked* and *spoke* with our first parents in the cool of the Garden of Eden's evenings. Imagine the Creator of every object, microbe, plant, and animal on earth and in the universe seeking a friendship and chat with one of His creations. He knew the capabilities of Adam and Eve since He had made them. He walked and talked with them in person in the garden. Imagine the conversations. What animals did you encounter today, Adam? What did you learn about earth today? How did you like that sunset, Eve? Glorious, wasn't it? God of the universe present with man.

Later, He displayed His presence to Moses in a burning bush. Moses was out of God's will, away from his mission in Egypt and keeping someone else's sheep hidden on the backside of the desert. Yet Almighty God wanted to be with Moses. So He caused a disturbance on the hillside—a fire that didn't consume the bush. It got Moses' attention, and suddenly Moses was on holy ground with the one and only God.

When Israel was set free from slavery in Egypt and began their journey across the wilderness, God showed up as a pillar of smoke and fire at night and as a glorious cloud that covered the Tabernacle in the daytime. He never left them to wander alone—no matter how many times they rebelled and sinned against Him. His presence was always there.

Later the prophet Elijah fled Jezebel and hid in the desert, feeling alone and forgotten. He even cried out that he was the only prophet left. And when God saw how despondent and depressed Elijah was, God showed up in the sound of a gentle whisper.

In the New Testament, when the disciples thought all was lost because the Master had been crucified and when it looked like the enemy had won and they had believed a lie, Jesus appeared on the shore cooking breakfast and offering words of comfort and joy in His presence.

On the Day of Pentecost, God sent His Holy Spirit to comfort and empower the new church so that the Gospel could be carried to the ends of the earth.

When we need Him, He shows up. His presence is real and offers comfort and power in our lives each day. We cannot live without His presence.

God's presence shines His light into our hearts and reveals what might be hidden. In fact, one of the ways we know we are in His presence is how He lights up the known and unknown thoughts, attitudes, and rebellion of our hearts. In His presence, we are more aware of what pleases Him. If we want to follow Him, then we must also want and pray for His presence.

Oswald Chambers said, "Having the reality of God's presence is not dependent on our being in a particular circumstance or place. But is only dependent on our determination to keep the Lord before us continually." In this statement, Chambers confirms the idea that if we want to know God's presence, we can. He is willing. He is waiting. He is available to us.

Scripture has provided us a spiritual framework to invite God's presence into our lives. We can invoke His "Jehovah-compound names." These are names that underscore His characteristics and note manifestations of His power and sovereignty. Throughout the scriptures, those names are expressed in praise—expressions of thanks for His miraculous intervention in past crises, gratitude for rescue, strength and guidance in the present, and faith He will show up in the future.

I have found a dozen of these in my Bible readings and I have learned to pray these names into and over my life.

Jehovah-Tsidkenu (Jeremiah 23:6): The Lord my Righteousness

Jehovah-Makeddesh (Leviticus 20:8) The Lord my Sanctifier

Jehovah-Shalom (Judges 6:24) The Lord my Peace

Jehovah-Shammah (Exodus 48:35 and Psalm 139:7-10) The Lord Ever-present

Jehovah-Yireh (Genesis 22:14) The Lord my Provider

Jehovah-Rophe (Exodus 15:26) The Lord my Healer

Jehovah-Nissi (Exodus 17:15) The Lord my Banner of Victory

Jehovah-Raah (Psalm 23:1) The Lord my Shepherd

Jehovah-Tsuri (Psalms 18:1-2 and 144:1-2) The Lord my Rock

Jehovah-Tsebaoth (1 Samuel 17:45) The Lord of Hosts

Jehovah-Malek (Psalms 5:2, 44:4) The Lord my King

Jehovah-Shaphat (Judges 11:27 and Psalm 75:7) The Lord my Judge

You may wonder how to pray these Jehovah compound-names. For me it sounds like this.

Lord, You are my *Jehovah Tsidkenu*—my righteousness. Without Your perfect life on earth, Your sacrifice on the cross, and Your resurrection, I would be condemned by my sin and face death eternal. But You are my righteousness. Thank You for saving my soul.

Lord, you are my Jehovah-Makeddesh—my sanctifier. You come into my life and help me make right choices and turn from sin. You purify my life and conform me into Your image.

Lord, You are my *Jehovah-Shalom*—my peace. In this world of chaos and trouble, there is no peace or calm or goodwill. You alone are peace that passes all understanding.

Lord, You are my Jehovah-Shammah-ever present. I am never alone because You walk beside me. You live in my heart and direct my paths. I can depend on You.

Lord, you are my Jehovah-Yireh—my provider. I will never worry about food or shelter or finances because when there seems to be no way, You always show up with just what I need. I trust in You.

Lord, you are *Jehovah-Rophe*—my healer. No matter what the diagnosis, I will trust You because You are the great physician. I need not worry about disease because You are in control and my ultimate destination is to be with You.

Lord, you are *Jehovah-Nissi*—my banner of victory. When I struggle with defeat, You are the winner of every battle. You are the conquering hero of my life.

Lord, you are *Jehovah-Raah*—my shepherd. Lead me into green pastures and still waters. Restore my soul. Give me rest and peace.

Lord, you are *Jehovah-Tsuri*—my rock. I will not falter or fail because You are my rock of ages. My strength and strong tower. I trust in You.

Lord, you are *Jehovah-Tsebaoth*—The Lord of hosts. You are the creator and sustainer of life. You alone have control of all. You are trustworthy.

Lord, you are *Jehovah-Malek*—my king. I worship You. You deserve all honor and praise.

Lord, you are *Jehovah-Shaphat*—my judge. I can trust you to defend and correct me. I will not take matters into my hands, but I will trust You as my judge. As I speak and praise Your names in prayer You write Your name upon me and envelop me. Fill me and cover me with Your presence.

A wonderful result of seeking the presence of the Lord through His names is that the exercise is not a one-way experience. We are *adoring,* as well as inviting and calling upon, the attributes of God. This adoration of ours is returned in His love and acceptance.

Psalm 22:3 tells us that God *"inhabits"* the praises of His people. Other translations use terms such as "enthrones" or "sit upon" the praises.

From such praise comes the presence of the Holy Spirit. You not only can *believe* in it; you often may *feel* it. When we personally declare and praise His names, His presence fills us. There is no way to overestimate the effect of recognizing our blessings and our reasons for faith when we specifically embrace the Lord's attributes and invite Him to operate in us.

Every true child of God wants to have righteousness guide our thoughts and actions and to be sanctified (made holy) in the Lord's sight. We long for His peace to permeate us, knowing that He is ever-present in, through and around us; and that He will always provide our needs and heal us physically and spiritually.

We thrill at the Lord's promises of victory as we strive to live the Gospel, and we trust that He will shepherd us through valleys and lead us to mountain tops. We cling to Him as our rock and our fortress when we are assailed by enemies in the flesh or of the spirit.

God's children rejoice that He is the Lord of Hosts who calls upon the angelic armies in defense of His people and to defeat Satan. He is our King, the One in charge of our past, present, and future.

"Praise is the portal to the presence of God."
~David Brazzeal

Reflections

Do you long for God's presence in your life? How will you now pray asking for His presence?

Describe how praying the names of God might help you seek His presence?

Which name means the most to you today and why?

Does any one of the names seem impossible in your current situation? Explain your answer.

Spend time in prayer asking for God's presence.

4

Seeking His Power

"Our high and privileged calling is to
do the will of God in the power of
God for the glory of God."
~J. I. Packer

Praying in the power of God is the critical catalyst to make our prayers eternally effective. As human beings, we can produce positive accomplishments through good intentions and good efforts. However, nothing good that truly lasts can be accomplished without God's power.

The Apostle Paul relied on God's power in all aspects of life and ministry.

"I was with you in weakness and in fear and much trembling, and my speech and my message were not in plausible words of wisdom, but in demonstration of the Spirit and of power, so that your faith might not rest in the wisdom of men but in the power of God" (1 Corinthians 2:3-5 ESV).

Paul knew that God is our eternal power source.

"For God, who said, 'Let light shine out of darkness,' has shone in our hearts to give the light of the knowledge of the glory of God in the face of Jesus Christ. But we have this treasure in jars of clay, to show that the surpassing power belongs to God and not to us" (2 Corinthians 4:6-7 ESV).

Further, Ephesians 5:17-18 (ESV) urges us to "not be foolish, but understand what the will of the Lord is," clearly identifying that as continually being "filled with the Spirit."

The source of God's power in us is His Holy Spirit. When we are filled with the Holy Spirit daily, our prayers are filled with power.

Let's try to understand this element of power in our prayers by understanding what happened to us when we accepted Jesus as our personal Savior. John the Baptist said, "I myself did not know Him but [God] who sent me to baptize with water said to me, 'He on whom you see the Spirit descend and remain, this is He who baptizes with the Holy Spirit'" (John 1:33).

The one on whom the Spirit descended is Jesus and when we believe and receive Him, we are given the power of the Holy Spirit in our lives and especially in our prayers. As we yield ourselves to the Holy Spirit, we are indwelled and given power from the Holy Spirit. We ask daily to be completely filled with His power.

I believe God provided Old Testament imagery for this New Testament spiritual imperative to seek His power through the Holy Spirit. In Exodus 25:31-39, God gave instructions to Moses for the *Menorah,* a seven-stemmed golden lampstand fueled by the purest olive oil. As you pray for power, visualize the *menorah,* assigning one candlestick stem each to the characteristics of the seven-fold Spirit of God as found in Isaiah:

Spirit of the Lord – Supernatural power

Spirit of wisdom – Supernatural thoughts

Spirit of understanding – Supernatural clarity

Spirit of counsel – Supernatural ability to make wise choices

Spirit of might – Supernatural strength

Spirit of knowledge – Supernatural ability to hear God's voice

Spirit of the fear of the Lord – Supernatural reverence of God

"The Spirit of the Lord will rest on Him—the Spirit of wisdom and of understanding, the Spirit of counsel and of might, the Spirit of the knowledge and fear of the Lord" (Isaiah 11:2 NLT).

The power of the Holy Spirit in our prayers helps us face any situation, knowing that with God nothing is impossible. With the power of the Holy Spirit, believing for healing, deliverance, direction, and guidance becomes natural like breathing.

When I was in my early twenties, I was a newly married graduate student at UCLA and had just begun a Christian walk along with my wife. We were attending a church in Sherman Oaks, and even though we were inexperienced Christians, my wife and I were asked to become the high-school youth leaders. We agreed but felt extremely inadequate in helping the youth with their many problems. In the weeks before we accepted this leadership position, my mom had sent a letter encouraging me and my wife to seek the baptism in the Holy Spirit. She basically told us that we needed God's power to accomplish the things that God had planned for us. I had seen how this experience had changed my mom's Christian walk, but really did not understand much about this experience.

One of the troubled youth in our group attended a prayer meeting in someone's home and was saved and baptized in the Holy Spirit during the meeting. We saw a dramatic difference in this young man's life. A week later, we attended the same prayer meeting. Person after person shared how God had intervened in their lives during the previous week—answered prayers, wisdom for difficult situations, sharing the Gospel with others, miracles, and life transformations. As I listened to these reports, I wanted experiences like these. After the meeting, my wife and I approached the leader and confessed that we felt something was missing in our Christian walk. The leader told us that we needed to be baptized in the Holy Spirit. He asked if he and his wife could pray for us. We agreed, and they took us to a private room in the house. They then led us in a prayer asking for God to fill us with His Holy Spirit. After the prayer, tears rolled down my cheeks as I experienced what seemed like the windows of God's love and power being poured out on me. My wife's experience was similar and yet unique to her. Each of us felt God's power and we both received the gift of tongues, which proved to be a powerful tool in our prayer lives. I began to devour the Bible and experience a greater revelation about what I was reading. I felt new courage and shared the Gospel message with each of my friends in the UCLA graduate school.

This experience was the beginning of praying in power and my prayer life seemed to grow in leaps and bounds. I have also come to understand that God wants us to be continually filled with His Holy Spirit according to Ephesians 5:18.

A number of years ago, I began to ask every day for God to fill me with His Holy Spirit. My daily prayer for God's power sounds like this: *"Lord, I seek Your power in my life this day. I ask You to fill me with Your seven-fold Spirit – the Spirit the Lord, of wisdom, of understanding, of counsel, of might, of knowledge, and of the fear of the Lord.*

When we pray daily for the filling of the Spirit, we receive power, and we set ourselves up for God to work in and through us. The English evangelist, Smith Wigglesworth said, "The power of God will take you out of your own plans and put you into the plan of God." If you want to pray with the power of God and allow Him to direct your life, then seek the power of the Holy Spirit daily.

The Holy Spirit bestows gifts on believers so that we can function in His power on earth. Those gifts are for the common good, and the Holy Spirit may empower you with one of these gifts today so that you can lead others to the Kingdom. Paul wrote,

"To each is given the manifestation of the Spirit for the common good. For to one is given through the Spirit the utterance of wisdom, and to another the utterance of knowledge according to the same Spirit, to another faith by the same

Spirit, to another gifts of healing by the one Spirit, to another the working of miracles, to another prophecy, to another the ability to distinguish between spirits, to another various kinds of tongues, to another the interpretation of tongues" (1 Corinthians 12:7-12 ESV).

These gifts fall into three categories: *Vocal* (tongues, interpretation of tongues, and prophecy), *Supernatural* (healing, miracles, and faith), and *Revelation* (the word of knowledge, the word of wisdom, and the discerning of spirits).

As I have prayed and asked God to use me in these gifts as He sees fit, I have seen God move in powerful ways. Let me share just a few examples to encourage you:

I was in a gathering of other believers and was seated next to a missionary to Kenya, East Africa. During the meeting, I felt a strong prompting that I was to share with the missionary that God greatly loved him. I was reluctant since I had never done something like this before. I told the Lord that if this was Him prompting me, then I wanted Him to have the person sitting on the other side of me to bump me in the ribs with his elbow. Immediately, that person bumped me in the ribs with his elbow. To say the least I was shocked. I then spoke to the missionary about the great love God had for him…he seemed to be very blessed with the words I had shared.

On another occasion, I was sharing with my mom about seeing a miracle when a person was prayed for who had a leg shorter than the other. I told her how I had seen the short leg lengthen during a prayer. Mom told me one of her legs was shorter than the other…she had to have the length of her pants legs adjusted differently for each leg. Mom asked if I would pray for her. I gulped, and then prayed for her short leg to lengthen. As I prayed, I watched her leg lengthen miraculously. Later, she told me that she had to have all her pants readjusted so the hems were the same.

On a trip to Honduras a number of years ago, I was to speak in a church during a Sunday service. I had a very strong impression a few days before the gathering that I was to speak on healing and then pray for people who needed healing. At the end of the service, my eyes were drawn like a magnet to a man in the back of the sanctuary who was in a wheelchair. I walked back to him and had another impression that I was to ask him to let me help him walk. It was a difficult journey to the front of the sanctuary and back to the wheelchair as his legs half walked and his feet dragged on the floor. I prayed for him the whole time we were walking for healing. When I helped him into his wheelchair, I wondered if there had been any healing in this man's body. I moved on to praying for others and saw God move in some wonderful ways, but the man in the wheelchair was foremost on my mind. Later that evening, I was talking to the pastor and asked about the man in the wheelchair. I told him that I so wanted God to touch him with healing. The pastor told me that God had done so. First of all, the man had not previously been able to move his legs, and it was a miracle that he could half-walk and drag his feet with my help. Further, at the end of the meeting, the man told his wife that he believed he could walk without any help to the car. She was shocked and told him that was impossible. The man proceeded to stand and then walked to the car without any help! His wife brought the wheelchair.

While sharing with the Commander of the Honduran Army about leadership, I was asked to pray for this leader. As I walked over to pray with him, the Lord gave me a word of wisdom that I was to first share about becoming a Christian with this leader. He was Catholic, and God gave me incredible wisdom as I shared the plan of salvation. I was amazed at how God gave me words to share that were so unique to his background and situation. When I finished sharing, I asked him if he would like to receive Jesus as his Savior and Lord. Tears began to form in his eyes, as he said, "yes." He received Christ as his Savior and Lord. After praying for this man, the Lord gave me a personal word for him…if he would be a leader with integrity, God would promote him to be the Commander of Honduras' armed forces. Less than a year after praying with me, he was appointed as the Commander of the Armed Forces of Honduras. Out of that meeting, the general and I became good friends, and he asked me to share with his subordinate leaders and troops on many occasions.

Will God give you every gift every day—tongues, interpretation, prophecy, healing, miracles, faith, revelations of knowledge, insights of holy wisdom, and being able to identify foes in spiritual warfare? Perhaps not, but He will give you every tool and power you need for each life situation. Pray that He will empower you. Be open and willing for any of His empowering gifts. He prepares us for battle.

"When the power of God is present, healing
and deliverance are just like breathing!"
~T. B. Joshua

Reflections

Have you ever asked the Lord to fill you with His Holy Spirit?

What happened in your spiritual life when you asked Him?

Did you sense His power fill you?

Did the Word open up in a new way?

Did you receive the gift of tongues (see 1 Corinthians 14)?

Did your love for Jesus increase?

If you have never asked for God to fill you with His Holy Spirit, are you willing to do so right now?

Are you willing to pray every day for God to fill you with His Holy Spirit, using the list from Isaiah 11:2?

Have you ever asked God to use you in the nine supernatural gifts listed in 1 Corinthians 12:7-12? Describe what happened.

If you are unsure about the filling of the Holy Spirit, I suggest you read this book: *The Overflowing Power of the Holy Spirit* by Jack Hayford. It is a very balanced and informative book that will greatly help you.

5

Seeking His Protection

"A God wise enough to create me
and the world I live in is wise enough
to watch out for me."
~Philip Yancey

We are at war. I'm not talking about the dozens of ongoing armed conflicts that rage worldwide at any given time, claiming many thousands of lives. Our warfare, the warfare of the believer, is a different kind of battle. Our warfare is spiritual. Our victories and setbacks are seen in the temporal (earthly) realm as lives are changed and futures are rescued. But our battles also have *eternal* consequences.

Paul wrote, "For though we walk in the flesh, we are not waging war according to the flesh. For the weapons of our warfare are not of the flesh but have divine power to destroy strongholds" (2 Corinthians 10:3-4 ESV).

One of the weapons that God gives us to fight the battle is prayer. And Paul spoke resolutely about believers being able to depend on God's protection, using the metaphor of armor.

More than 2,000 years later, the concept of armor remains helpful to us. No matter how advanced the technology of modern warfare, soldiers still go into battle with helmets and armor.

"Finally, be strong in the Lord and in the strength of His might. Put on the whole armor of God, that you may be able to stand against the schemes of the devil. For we do not wrestle against flesh and blood, but against the rulers, against the authorities, against the cosmic powers over this present darkness, against the spiritual forces of evil in the heavenly places. Therefore take up the whole armor of God, that you may be able to withstand in the evil day, and having done all, to stand firm. Stand therefore, having fastened on the belt of truth, and having put on the breastplate of righteousness, and, as shoes for your feet, having put on the readiness given by the gospel of peace. In all circumstances take up the shield of faith, with which you can extinguish all the flaming darts of the evil one; and take the helmet of salvation, and the sword of the Spirit, which is the word of God, praying at all times in the Spirit, with all prayer and supplication" (Ephesians 6:10-18 ESV).

When we stand before the Lord to "take up the whole armor of God," it is helpful to physically imagine putting on the armor. I start at my head and work my way down, putting on the pieces Paul described, one by one. I pray aloud:

"Lord, I put on the helmet of salvation," touching my head.

"Lord, I thank You for prayer in the spirit," touching my lips and mouth.

"Lord, I take the shield of faith above all, that stops every fiery dart of the enemy," strapping it onto my arm.

"Lord, I grip the sword of the Spirit, which is your Word," holding the Bible up as my sword.

"Lord, I put on the breastplate of righteousness," touching my chest.

"I belt my waist with truth," tying it around my middle.

Finally, when I reach my feet, I think about how soldiers wear tough boots to meet the challenges of rough terrain. In Paul's time, sandals or heavily laced leather boots fit that role; the idea is the same—protection for the march ahead. So, once more I get my body involved, moving my feet into the heavenly footwear. I pray, *"Lord, I thank You for preparing and covering my feet with the Gospel of peace."*

How does this armor help us? Let's consider each part of the garment. First the helmet of salvation. A helmet is vital for the soldier to protect the brain and eyes and mouth. Our helmet of salvation protects us in that same way. Our thoughts are protected so that we never doubt the God of our salvation, and we don't turn from Him to other gods. The helmet protects our eyes helping us focus on the power and promises of God not on our circumstances. Our mouth is protected so that we don't take in the dust and filth of this world. (See 2 Corinthians 10:5).

Prayer is a powerful piece of our armor. God wants to empower our prayers with the Holy Spirit. Just pray, believe, and leave the results to God. This piece of armor is limitless in its impact!

When we strap on the shield of faith, we cover our vulnerable parts with trust. The Roman shield was as large as a door and covered the warrior. The enemy may send arrows that would harm our ability to function or damage our ability to move forward. But when we use our shield, confident in Jesus and depending on Him because we believe Him, we are protected (see Hebrews 1:1, 6).

The sword of the Spirit is the Word of God. A sword is used offensively. The Bible is our offensive weapon against the enemy. Just as Jesus used individual verses during the time when Satan tempted Him, we can also use individual verses. If we are tempted to lie, we should quote Colossians 3:9, "Do not lie to each other, since you have taken off your old self with its practices." When tempted to gossip, instead quote, "Do not let any unwholesome talk come out of your mouths, but only what is helpful for building others up according to their needs, that it may benefit those who listen" (Ephesians 4:29). When feeling like a failure, quote, "I have been crucified with Christ and I no longer live, but Christ lives in me. The life I now live in the body, I live by faith in the Son of God, who loved me and gave himself for me" Galatians 2:20. The Word of God has the answer for every situation we may face.

A typical Roman soldier wore a covering made of bronze or chain over his chest. This piece of equipment protects the vital organs, especially the heart. The breastplate of the believer is righteousness, which was purchased by Jesus on the cross. Our heart is guarded by the pure, precious blood of Jesus. (See Matthew 6:33).

Jesus said, "I am the way, the truth, and the life" (John 14:6). He is truth. All truth and nothing but the truth. When we tie on the belt of truth, we are putting all our faith in the truth of Jesus. He is the answer to all life's problems and the key to joy and peace and life eternal.

Putting on the shoes of the Gospel of peace means that we are ready for battle. These shoes help us stand firm in our confidence in Jesus and help us move through the world offering the gift of peace (salvation) to each person we meet. When we speak to others about Him, we are wearing the shoes. It is important that we never take off the shoes but continually share the Gospel. (See 2 Timothy 2:15).

Pray each day as you put on the armor of God.

Sometimes the protection of God is so evident, it is easy to recognize it and offer thanksgiving. When you barely miss a car on the freeway. When you don't catch the flu that seems to have struck everyone around you. When you receive an unexpected check in the mail—just in time. We love to praise God for intervening in our life with shelter, safety, and provision. But there are other situations when God protected you and you didn't know it. When you left your house a few minutes late and avoided a car accident. When He helped your child make a wise decision. He is protecting us in every situation, and we may never know the extent of His shield around us.

We may pray for wealth or safety or deliverance from calamity, but God doesn't always answer those prayers because He knows best. Samuel wrote, "The Lord sends poverty and wealth; He humbles and He exalts" (1 Samuel 2:7). Sometimes He allows us to face trouble and trials because He knows that we will grow strong spiritually by learning to trust Him. And if we could see the final result that would happen if He answered all our prayers, we would understand why He sometimes says, "no."

The Psalms of David are filled with prayers for protection and praises for the times God protected the shepherd-king. Read Psalms 112:1-3 and 1 Chronicles 17:16-27.

The prayers for protection that we pray fall into several categories. The first is praying for personal protection. We need to pray for ourselves because the enemy is alive and watching for any chance to harm us. *God protect me from evil images from TV, the Internet, or printed materials so that my mind will stay focused on you. Lord, give me strength to resist the enemy when temptation looms. Surround me with your shield of protection.*

The second category is praying for our family and others. Pray for a hedge around your kids and spouse and extended family. *Lord, protect my children and grandchildren from emotional attacks. Help them understand and reject wrong or harmful teaching in the school. Give them an ear for the truth. Shelter my loved ones from the arrows of the enemy.*

Another way to pray for protection is to ask for blessing. God's protection includes His loving kindness and gifts of hope, peace, and joy. *Lord, I ask You to shower us with blessings that will keep our hearts pure. Fill us with Your love and joy. Press Your peace into our hearts. Help us grab the hope that only comes from You.*

Your prayer time is the most important part of your day. Your prayers are protection for you.

"Prayer is a strong wall and fortress of the
church; it is a godly Christian weapon."
~Martin Luther

Reflections

Have you experienced a spiritual attack against you, a family member, or a friend? What was your reaction?

Have you studied or heard a message about the armor of God?

What did you learn?

Have you prayed the armor of God? Describe your prayer.

Describe a time when you knew that God protected you and your family.

Write a prayer for personal protection.

Write a prayer for the protection of your family.

Write a prayer for God's blessings.

A Final Word
What Remains?

What remains? Your commitment to prayer. Praying regularly and fervently will change your life and energize your service to the Lord. Prayer brings incredible victories and blessings for you and your family when you tap into our Eternal Source with awe, reverence, and awareness of our divinely-created role in His plan.

Praying the five prayer principles takes about ten minutes. That's less than the time you wait for your double-shot latte at your favorite over-priced coffee shop. You can pray for ten minutes each day and forever change your life.

Ten minutes to touch the heart of your Creator; ten minutes for God to change your life. It is time to wake up, to be alert, and to be aware that the Lord's coming is nearer, every day.

It is time, as Peter urged, to consider *"what sort of people ought you to be in lives of holiness and godliness"* (2 Peter 3:11 ESV) and to act on those revelations, while we can.

Being connected devotionally to God is the key. The Lord gave me this prayer template to help me connect to Him. I believe it will do that same for you.

Will you do it?

PRAYER GUIDE

5 Life-Changing Principles for Prayer

Seek His Purity

Ask God to search your heart and reveal any sin (Psalm 139:23-24)

Welcome His instruction and correction in your life (Proverbs 3:11-12 & 4:13)

Pray for

> Love, joy, peace, gentleness, goodness, faithfulness, longsuffering, kindness, and self-control.

Seek His Purpose

Present your body to Him each morning (Romans 12:1)

Choose the fear of the Lord for your life (Proverbs 1:29-30)

Pray the prayer of Jabez for you and your family (1 Chronicles 4:9-10)

Bless us indeed; enlarge our territory; keep Your Hand upon us; and keep us from evil.

Seek His Presence

Ask for God to cover your life with His Jehovah-compound names revealed in Scripture. Praise and thank God for each of the following names:

The Lord my Righteousness (Tsidkenu) (Jeremiah 23:6)

The Lord my Sanctifier (Makeddesh) (Ezekiel 20:12)

The Lord my Peace (Shalom) (Jude 6:24)

The Lord Ever-present (Shammah) (Exodus 25:8 & Psalm 139:7-10)

The Lord my Provider (Yireh) (Genesis 22:14)

The Lord my Healer (Rophe) (Exodus 15:26)

The Lord my Banner of Victory (Nissi) (Exodus 17:15)

The Lord my Shepherd (Raah) (Psalm 23:1)

The Lord my Rock (Tsuri) (Psalm 144:1)

The Lord of Hosts (Tsebaoth) (1 Samuel 17:45)

The Lord my King (Malek) (Psalm 5:2; 44:4)

The Lord my Judge (Shaphat) (Deuteronomy 32:36; Is 33:22)

Seek His Power

Pray to be filled with the Holy Spirit each day (Ephesians 5:18)

Use the pattern in Isiah 11:1-2. Pray for God's 7-fold Spirit to fill you: Spirit of the Lord; Spirit of wisdom; Spirit of understanding; Spirit of counsel; Spirit of might; Spirit of knowledge; and Spirit of the fear of the Lord.

Ask for God's gifts to operate in your life today (1 Corinthians 12:7-10)

> <u>Vocal:</u> tongues, interpretation of tongues, and prophesy
> <u>Supernatural:</u> healings, miracles, and faith
> <u>Revelation:</u> the word of knowledge, the word of wisdom, and discerning of spirits

Seek His Protection

Ask God to protect you with the armor of God (Eph 6:10-18)

Put on God's armor, piece by piece, starting at the top of your head:
> The helmet of salvation
> Prayer and supplication in the Spirit
> The shield of faith above all
> The sword of the Spirit which is His Word
> The breastplate of righteousness
> The belt of truth
> The Gospel of peace on your feet

<u>Pray For:</u>

Your family members by name (blessing, health, salvation, etc.)

Your church, pastor, and church leaders

Your workplace, boss and fellow workers

The school and the teachers for you and your children

Government leaders:

The president and your state governor

Your senators or representatives (national and state)

Your mayor and city officials

Personal or family needs

Other important people and aspects of your life

ABOUT THE AUTHOR

Stu Johnson is the Executive Administrator, overseeing the day to day matters for Grace International Churches and Ministries, Inc. This ministry encompasses more than 3,000 churches in more than 100 countries. Stu has extensive ministry experience as a conference speaker, youth pastor, college and career pastor, associate pastor, senior pastor, and district superintendent. He was also an Air Force officer for 30 years, retiring in 1999 as a Colonel. In his final Air Force command, he led an organization of almost 6,000 military and civilians with 30 subordinate commands. He is married to Debbe and has 2 grown children, Andrew, a vice principal of a school, and Lisa, a medical doctor, and three grandchildren.

Endnotes

Bruce Wilkerson, The Prayer of Jabez, 2000, Multnomah Publishers, Inc., p 44